Shortcut To A
Nervous Breakdown

Shortcut To A Nervous Breakdown

Erick K. Huling

Library of Congress Control Number:		2010918242
ISBN:	Hardcover	978-1-4568-3060-1
	Softcover	978-1-4568-3059-5
	Ebook	978-1-4568-3061-8

All photography in this book, including the cover and author photo, is by my very talented nephew, Joshua Huling.

Joshua is a graduate of the Hallmark Institute of Photography in Turners Falls, Massachusetts, where he studied under the renowned photographer, Gregory Heisler.

This book was printed in the United States of America.

To order additional copies of this book, contact:
Xlibris Corporation
1-888-795-4274
www.Xlibris.com
Orders@Xlibris.com
90375

Contents

Shortcut To A Nervous Breakdown
is dedicated to my mom,
Geraldine Esther Trimble Huling.
I love you mom.

Chapter One

LIFE

A Twinkle In Her Eye

Since I was a twinkle in mother's eye,
Since the night I dreamed that I could fly,
Since Love begat life and then desire,
I've needed something to take me higher.
Mother said Jesus! with a lot of fire.

A long time ago, in a real small town—
We had a blinking red light, 'til they took it down.
My mother would hold me when I was scared—
I wouldn't let go 'til a story she'd shared.
Not a word was wasted, not a poem spared.

I had my favorite, it was about me.
Before I was born, I was meant to be.
My mother would smile and hold me tight.
She'd tell me everything would be alright.
Then she'd tell me a story about this little light.

I would close my eyes and imagine a time,
A time before time, before rhythm and rhyme.
Mother and Father had four little boys,
No need for another, they had so many joys—
But mother knew of Jesus' ploys.

When she was just a young pretty lass,
She would stare into her mom's looking glass
And dream of our family, and through prayer,
She knew of her fate by the twinkles there.
A quintet of stars resided her stare!

Bin Laden's Tears

Unforgiving tears fall from her American
Eyes, onto her swollen belly. Her unborn
Child kicks, restlessly awaiting a fatherless
Life—because of extremist Islamic terrorists?
How do you explain that to an eleven year old?
She worries.
A strangely calming lullaby
Makes its way like whispered morphine
Into her upset womb,
And soothes her only hope.

Who will cry Bin Laden's tears?
For he cannot, whose eyes are spears,
Whose hands are guns,
Whose thoughts are bombs,
Who kills our fathers and our moms.
Who will cry Bin Laden's tears?
Whose soul has dried through hatred's years.
When he's consumed in Hell's brimstone
And reaches up so all alone
For Abraham to quench his thirst,
Who will cry Bin Laden's tears?

Fingernail Moon

A fingernail moon
Rides a strawberry sunset—
In winter's foreplay.

Kamping With Kelton

The stars shake glitter o'er the trees,
A symphony of crickets, please!
My niece and her son sleeping still
Inside the tent, I've climbed this hill.
For sleep or peace patiently waiting,
The pale moonlight slowly sedating.
Memories of Kelton fishing
For grasshoppers, quickly swishing.
"My gwasshopper! Uggitt, see?"
The street-lamp moon helping me.
"My caught gwasshopper, mommy!"
Kelton screams to her, from me.
Jes praises her son's hard work.
"My pwoud of you!" She loves that quirk.
He'll soon learn the way we talk,
The way we cry, the way we walk.
But for now, he just turned three,
Amusing, and impressing me.

Cancun

I miss the white sand between my toes.
I miss the bright blue ocean
Crashing over my head.
I miss the feeling I had—free, oh so free.
I miss everything, but most of all I miss me,
In Cancun.

I hold a seashell up close to my ear—
I see a postcard of that beautiful place.
I close my tired eyes—
I see palm trees swaying in the breeze.
I hear the ocean saying, everything's cool,
In Cancun.

I remember all of the good times—
Club Las Velas, the food, and the songs.
I remember Wendell and I laughing along.
Nobody knows who you are, they said.
So unwind, and have a good time,
In Cancun.

A Well Writ Poem

Every word has once been writ,
Every thought has once been thunk—
All the while, though done before,
I still write and think up junk.

To my amazement, pure and simple,
The words still rhyme, and so I write them.
Endless humans blink their eyes,
Maybe some day to read my poem.

Doors are opened, some slammed shut,
Just by reading a well writ poem.
Words that have been used for years,
Arranged just so, and fed cerebrum.

This is not a well writ poem,
I'm just one guy that loves to write them.
Thinking thoughts and typing madly,
Simply trying to pen this whim.

Giving In To Helplessness

Giving in to helplessness—
Is that my cure, or recklessness?
My reality—incumbent fantasy.
Not being there—lunacy.
Trouble comes as fantasy turns
To reality. My heart yearns.
My mind blends fact and fiction.
Fantasy blooms addiction.
I watch myself just like a ghost
Do things undreamable for most.
Then wake up in that lowly state
Of helplessness, and then debate
The cure, or likelihood of life
After addiction. And in my strife,
I must make that good decision—
Helplessness must be religion.

The Separating

It's tormenting, the separating.
Loyalties slowly deflating,
Foreshadowing cremation.
Death beginning preparation,
Burning bridges of creation.

I see your shadow burning.
Fate has its way of turning
Friend against friend.
No longer to defend—
Only hate seems to mend.

Fusing what once was known
With something overblown.
In a fog as dark as night,
Tears stream down my sight—
Fear gripping my heart tight.

Insensitivity barricades
Itself in the Everglades.
Pushing hope away and waiting.
Harsh words are ever grating—
It's tormenting, the separating.

Blue Shades

Layered in blue shades,
Like thirty years of living—
Spring clouds at sunset.

Anger, In Full Bloom

In this requited anger,
Eyes wide open,
Teeth clinched shut.

His soul slips perilously
Through this dark tunnel of snakes.
Nothing else matters
But that his enemy quakes.

Wild anger produces branches
Of destruction and lies.
Forces out communication,
Fills the void with what belies.

Shrugged into isolation,
His tears fall silent, cold.
When she approaches,
Kindness retreats—new anger bold.

The betrayal in his mind retold.
The shock still numbs of being sold.

Wary Of Lines

Wary of lines
That can be crossed—
Forgiving of lines
That would be.

Walking this line
Of unending faith—
Dreaming of lines
That should be.

Monotony

I am overwhelmed,
Flooded with monotony—
Need to change seasons.

Fluidly Falling

Fluidly falling, unless it's freezing,
Then floating freely, but oh! That is snow!
Fluidly falling, splashing life on earth.
Bringing thistlessness to thirsty masses.
Don't like umbrellas, for I like to feel
Cool drops on my face, unless it's freezing,
But wait! That is sleet! Can you hear the tink?
The tink-tink, tink-tink, against my glasses?
Fluidly falling, newly refreshing,
Revitalizing, and effervescent.
Often quite forceful, miniature bombs.
Pounding man made lakes 'til they overflow.
Fluidly falling, finding me grateful.

Cader Tater

Cader Tater needs no translator,
When there's huntin' to do, he'll see ya later.
He's headin' to Dinoco with his friend Tow Mater.
If there's mischief to do, he's the instigator.

He likes bows and arrows, and that's no jive.
He likes his dad's big tractor, which he loves to drive.
If there's work to be done, he's the first in line.
He'll expect to be helping and his work will shine.

He's the best mechanic in this here hollow,
And if his dad's going, Cade's sure to follow.
He's his constant shadow, and his loyal friend,
Whether there's cow's to brand, or fences to mend.

Cade loves to play army with his older brother,
Never misses a chance to be with his mother.
He loves her cooking, he's a culinary eater,
When I see them together, there's nothing sweeter.

I, Like A Tree

I, like a tree, unleafed, so bare.
Branches and crows betrothed.
Not dead, just dormant, in cold air—
A silhouette, red sunset clothed.

Left lonely on its highway curve,
A twisting, wind-warped cottonwood.
Branches free of pompous pride,
I, like a tree, misunderstood.

Bent by ice's stormy craft,
Combed north by strong Gulf winds.
Grown from the dust bowl's strident past,
Thrust up through rocky bends.

I, like a tree, with roots entrenched,
Searching deep within the earth.
Forever seeking, forever longing,
For that which most would say is worth.

Cotton Candy Clouds

Cotton candy pink
Clouds making my mouth water,
This winter evening.

Sea Story

Walking along a distant shore,
By an ocean dyed blue it would seem.
Gazing intently into the unknown,
Pausing for such a moment to dream.

Wanderlust or wander lost,
I would not seem to know—
For by chance a meeting there
In that sand as white as snow.

A sweeping glance of my glossy eyes . . .
As a silver capped wave of destiny
Unearthed a jewel from the bowels of the earth . . .
Beheld the beauty of our mother the sea.

A shell of a life that once was,
But still, it is just a shell.
Hold it to your ear just now,
Hear the story it has to tell.

It is amazing to me that even the sea
Has recorded her voice for all to hear.
Through this simple device known as a shell,
Bringing happiness and peace throughout the year.

Debtor's Rhyme

This debt is more than I can bear,
Causing joyful thoughts to swear.
Wearing thin my fragile prayer—
There seems to be no one to care.

Relationships asphyxiated
By this monster I've created.
Tears start to fall, heavy weighted—
Tears of pity, guilt inflated.

Incubus

Behind towering cumulus,
Dwelling in incubus—
Glimpses of sanity,
Caressing profanity.

Kissed Awake

I lay, unemboldened—
Dreamless, on my bed of doubt—
Waiting for that eternal kiss.
Tension flowers with black petals
Scream anecdotes of
Seclusional bliss.
Faint whispers from a
White hummingbird are
Whisked away in
Rush hour traffic.
Eighteen-wheeled destruction,
Like an eagle to the hare,
Is epidemic.

High atop the Black Mesa
A monument stands
Tribute to the highest
Point of freedom; lower,
In the dusty ravine,
Dinosaur tracks remain
Emblazoned, where once
Water flowed freely, and life.

Frogger

An emerald
Magic carpet ride.
A nervous eye.
A step aside.
Into the murk
Until I'm gone.
Back on its pad
Singing its song.

Autumn

Autumn is decay
In its most beautiful form—
Dying leaves rejoice!

Phantom Father

He bequeathed life at will,
Then deserted it with ignorance.
Left innocent children defenseless
To concoct for themselves an imaginary father
In a cruel, aggressive society
That demands an illusion of correctness.

He gave life to children,
Later cruelly shoving them
Into the distant, forgotten corners
Of his conscience.
He might have wished they had never been,
That he had never met their mother.
He gave life to children,
Then tried to take it back by ignoring them.

The children thought he was saying
That they were not worth the trouble.
What he was trying to say was . . .
Children, I cannot stand your mother.
He will always be in their lives . . .
As a father, or as a phantom.

I Wish You Were Never

Words flew out of our mouths
Like fish hooks on tournament day.
Each word grasped from the tackle
And cast in the most dangerous way.

The love in my father's eyes
Had a glazed and furious tint.
I just wanted to go to church,
But he would not take a hint.

Never mind the thundering storm,
The lightning, or baseball sized hail.
My mind was locked and loaded,
I would surely face the gale.

I was young and seventeen.
Nothing else mattered.
Why couldn't he see
That my soul was battered?

I yelled at him,
"I wish you weren't my dad!"
He yelled back,
You're the son I should never have had!"

I stole the keys to his car,
And sped off in his Chevy Chevette.
The stinging tears in this violent storm
And I should never have met.

He was just trying to protect me
From the dangerous storm.
Instead I had created one
More furious than norm.

As I arrived at church
After dodging through the hail,
Pastor could see my distress
And that my spirit was frail.

We prayed that Dad would understand,
That God's Will would be followed,
That I could be forgiven,
And that my pride would be swallowed.

The mentally tormenting ride home
Foreshadowed what was to come.
A stinging Russian Olive branch.
Life restricted for weeks plus some.

Chapter Two

LOVE

Mother's Day Roses

I saved my mom's Mother's Day roses—
One red, one white.
Dad grew them from the warm red earth.
He knew they'd be ready when the time was right—
Barring a tornado, or a month of night.

"The red rose is for my love", he said,
As he pinned it to her brand new dress.
For thirty years she'd stuck with this man,
Through heaven and hell and times of duress.
Moments like these were sweet caress.

"The white rose is for your mother", he said.
Her mother had passed on just months before.
It was too hard for mom to hold back the tears.
"I won't have my mom", she cried, "on this day anymore."
"You'll see her again", he said, "on that Crystal Sea shore."

They're now dried and brittle and falling apart,
I hold them softly, but they still crumble.
They're as beautiful as my mother's heart.
They're on the table so my thoughts will stumble—
I pray not a moment her presence I fumble.

An Unforgiving Rim

Loving you is like playing
An unforgiving rim.
The line of demarcation set,
The prospect dim.

The sun beats hot
Upon the asphalt court.
Gatorade sweats out—
Love's sweet retort.

I shoot the ball
Never just right.
The ball, like air.
My hands too light.

With cool sarcasm
You bounce the ball away.
You belly dance the net
In teasing sway.

Lucía

Touching the sky, knowing it touched you,
I took a breath, knowing you would too.
I felt a breeze, and sent it to find you.
It smiled and laughed as if it knew.

Seeing the ocean illuminated blue,
Overwhelmed, I added a tear or two.
I wondered if this vast ocean had a clue
Of what cruel miles separate us two.

I've never smoked or drank the hot black brew.
I did today. Just to feel close to you.
I said they were the cure for me and you.
The universal cure for all those blue.

Inside Myself

It's curious,
The way I fear
Love's chance encounter—
Cupid's spear.
Quite ludicrous
The way I hide
Inside myself
When you are near.

Crying And Dreaming

The smell of concrete mixed with rainwater.
Taillights reflecting—my sin growing nearer.
The lights of the city bear down on my window.
They look in upon me like I'm a TV show.
Sowing and reaping, loving and lying.
Wanting to know you, slowly dying.
My door is open, but please, don't come in.
I could not bear to create the sin.
What is this sin, but lust revealed
To he whose wounds remain unhealed?
The sound of your car as it speeds by me screaming.
I lay on the carpet, crying and dreaming.

Nine Mile Road

I'm here on Nine Mile Road,
Right up Nine Mile Creek.
Wishing my love had
Nine more lives.
Hoping she'll give me just
One more chance,
To say I'm sorry.
I'm so sorry.

I'm here on Nine Mile Road,
Right up Nine Mile Creek.
The nearest phone is nine minutes away.
I know that she'll be gone
Before I can say
That I am sorry.
I'm so sorry.
Please, just give me
One more chance.

She loved me so much.
I took her for granted.
Now she's gone forever,
And I'm up Nine Mile Creek.

Love

Love is . . .
The willingness
To die for someone,
But only after
Exhausting
All other efforts
To live for them.

Chapter Three

SPIRIT

Tree Shadows

Tree shadows falling softly
On the blacktop 'neath my way.
Gently, gently, to and fro',
Silhouetted branches sway.

Rhythmic shadows wooing calm
Caress my week-worn mind.
Slowly, yet assuredly,
My worries cease to grind.

The presence of the One I love
Emerges from a shadow.
"Where have you been so long gone,
I could not closely follow?"

Father, please forgive me,
For I know not why I leave You
In repose among the shadows,
While I try so hard to be You.

Tree shadows falling softly
On the blacktop 'neath my way.
Gently, gently, to and fro',
Silhouetted branches sway.

Conviction

Let conviction rule,
Let it be your tool.
Don't listen to the fool.
Conviction is a jewel.

Let conviction rule,
Let it be your tool.
When the Lord convicts you,
Let conviction rule.

Conviction is addiction
To the heart of Jesus Christ.
When you face temptation
And to sin you are enticed,
Be listening for that still small voice,
Don't ever tune it out.
I know you'll make the right choice,
So cast out all fear and doubt.

Underworld

Is there any way
It can be true?
That God in me
Can rescue you?
That there is life
After this death?
That there is love
Within this breath?

The piercing screams
Of yesterday,
Explode upon
A brand new day.
A flash in the mirror
Of a laughing child,
Running freely,
Running wild.

The Reason

Jesus, You are the reason.
The reason I have to live,
The reason I have to give—
My all for You, and I do.

Jesus, You are my only hope.
The hope I need to feel,
To feel that way again—
When You came in.
Into my heart, my soul, my mind.

Jesus, there is no other name
That I call on. When I'm happy
Or when I'm sad, You're always there.
Waiting patiently, arms open wide.

You wrap your words of wisdom
Around my aching heart.
You soothe my burning soul.
You mend my distracted ways,
You guide me to the light—
The light of Your word,
My sword that will not fail,
Through Heaven or through Hell.

Drainage Ditches

Fancy concrete drainage ditches
Line our modern highway systems.
There to drain away our glitches.
Pacify our inner bitches.

Predestination rants and raves.
Israel stops to talk of peace.
A Palestinian misbehaves.
Innocent blood creates new waves.

Control the flow, flow the control,
Toward the ocean we don't know.
May thunderstorms light up your soul.
Flood the ditches, pay the toll.

August droughts bring renewed fear.
A choir sings How Great Thou Art.
Fire and locust plagues are near.
Faith and hope and love are dear.

Seek your peace where peace was born.
Love your neighbor and yourself.
Resolve to whom your soul is sworn.
Join not with those from heaven torn.

Tornado Love

It was the tornado love of Jesus, that swept me off my feet—
Whirled me through this life, towards eternity.
I once was lost in sin, but through Jesus, I'm forgiven.
The tornado love of Jesus swept my sins away.

Here on earth, a tornado might be scary,
Even from a distance, its awesome power you'll feel.
But when it reaches you, it'll lift you off your feet,
Give you a high you've never felt before.

Before I met my savior, my soul was like a building.
Built on the sand, not structured well, had to be torn down.
Just like a tornado, He stormed into my life,
Tore down the walls that had me bound, set my feet on solid ground.

One day in church, I was praying at the altar,
When I began to feel that awesome power of God.
I began to get happy, started shouting and praising God!
While that tornado love of Jesus swept my cares away.

You might be thinking you've never felt like that before—
Let me tell you something you really need to know.
The Holy Spirit's waiting to cleanse your soul,
All you really need to do is give Him full control.

Rainy Mountain

Take me to Rainy Mountain,
Where the wind blows fierce
And the raindrops pierce my skin.

Natives dance around my soul,
My hungry, beaten, thirsty soul.
Desensitized by civilization, that
Imagined line of demarcation, pushed
So far back I cannot breathe,
In and out of conscience seethe.

Like the buffalo, I have been
Hunted and gunned down because
My free spirit would not be tamed
Or fenced in, becoming gaunt and thin.
So now I'm listless, walking slow and giftless
Through the highways that they have paved—
For their applause, I behaved.

I climb the rocky slope of Rainy Mountain—
Rediscover that Spirit fountain.
Raindrops pierce my thirsty soul, the prayers of
Those who have gone before bring me
Back from the brink of extinction.

Amber's Answer

As a child I asked God, why? Why even try, if Hell was certain?
To make the sky so blue, so pure, was pleasing to the soul—
To make someone like me, like you? He knew—He knew that Hell was certain.
The chance was there that one could fall. There was a chance, and that He knew.

I questioned the risk He took for us, for those lost in eternal flames.
God took that risk for you, for me. Why, I cried? Why even bother?
All knowing, all seeing, all powerful—How could He let one soul burn?

He knew His creation could suffer eternal. Were there no second thoughts
As He breathed that first eternal breath into His image He had molded of clay?
Knowing Adam could fail, we could fail, that everything could fail?

I asked the clergy, my face in ashes.
Their harsh reply—Never question God!
I asked my dear friend Amber Hillock.
Her answer simple, in angelic form—

Because He loved me, He took the risk.
Because He loved me, He knew me.
Because He loved me, He gave me the choice.

Green Grass

Green grass turns yellow,
When hidden from the sunlight—
The soul, like the grass.

Drowning Demons

Crawling naked under church pews
While deacons pass the plate—
Lust demons crawl through holy socks,
Longing to be just like God.

Cursed though, we must be cursed,
For here we are, naked again—
Imagination feeding the flames
Of frozen, still live church bodies.

Like a deer chased by headlights
Pants for the holy water—
Three preachers on a joyride
Pray for monetary salvation.

Singing Amazing Grace, How Great Thou Art,
Is there Room At The Cross for me?
When you all get to Heaven,
Make room at the Gates for me.

Eternal Sting

Do you free darkness in your night?
Link your joy with dreams of flight?
Do you lose God in darkened seams?
Or is your God not who He seems?

As fire steals your lung's last breath,
And love's deported at your death.
Fear not my friend what life may bring,
Fear death, and Hell's eternal sting.

Worry-Worry

Worry-worry, caughtcha cryin'.
Depression chamber, no use dyin'.
Friday's comin', bright sunshinin'.
Where's the joy? I'm not buyin'.
Everybody! Search for Zion!

Worry-worry, caughtcha cryin'.
A drug called sin, a cure for lyin'.
For a season, you'll be flyin'.
A skillet jewel, a bride sighin'.
Deliverance from death's designin'.

Worry-worry, caughtcha cryin'.
Sixpence for love, hugs for tryin'.
Tears for fears, on faith relyin'.
Oingo-boingo! From God shyin'.
You won't get far without love shinin'.

Hurricanes of Grace

I swam with the devil in the ocean blue,
Lost all hope in the church of You.
Hurricanes of grace while dying for hope,
Tornados of justice at the end of a rope.
Enveloped by beauty, surrounded by love,
Searching for answers belonging above.

I swam with the devil in the livid sea,
Lost all hope in the church of me.
Just like Paul in the Book of Acts,
The wicked flesh plays a soothing sax.
Look far beyond to the final goal.
Listen only to the Creator of soul.

I swam with the devil, he lied to me.
Lost all hope, but hope is free.

The Midnight Song

1st Corinthians 7:20—Inspired by Bro. Mark R. Little's Sermon on this passage.

What is your isolation?
Unwillingness? Unfruitfulness?
What is your desolation?

When barrenness knocks on your door,
Get a song in your heart.
Sing believer. Sing believer.

Pray in faith. Faithfully pray.
Don't let temptation
To murmur and complain
Drive the song from your heart.
Sing believer.

At the darkest hour
Of the darkest night.
When you feel you can't go on,
Sing believer. Sing believer.

At the valley of Bakkah, make it a well.
The rain will come and fill it full.
Then all will see His faithfulness.

Ulterior Gladness

Falling asleep with a sense of sadness,
Crawl into dreams with ulterior gladness.
Life half-lived, a melancholy tour.
Tomorrow's not yours. For that, no cure.
You sleep and you wake with the same old feeling,
Like you should be doing a lot more kneeling.

Asleep with sight,
Awakened blind.
Truth be true,
Though unkind.

For Those Who Never Will

In the fresh cool laundered morning,
While dew drops await the sunrise
On the gentle green of grass blades—
Where the serpent slithers, lies—
There's within a peaceful longing,
Rising in all hearts arisen—
Who have willed to seek him early,
And prepared their hearts to listen—

For there are those who never will—
And there are those in intercession.

Where the heavy cross was burdened,
And true disciples lost their way—
Where the rocks beneath the cross
Were covered in His Blood to their dismay—
The rocks cried out with joyful praises
When no one else on earth would dare—
To the One, the King, the Lord, I Am—
The rocks beneath the cross paid fare.

For there are those who never will—
But there are those in intercession.

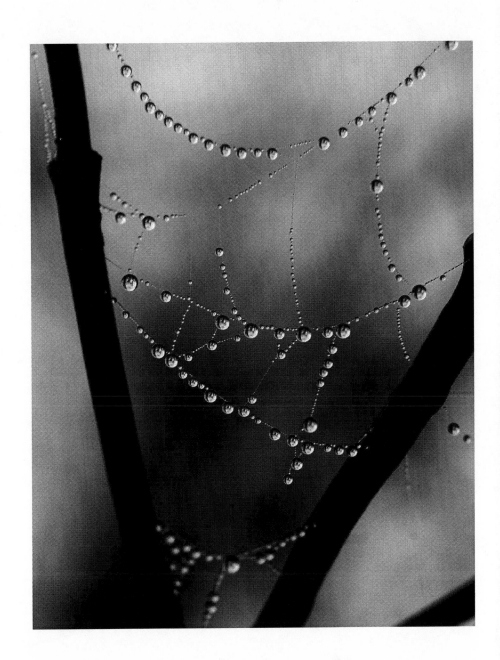

Pang Of Guilt

This pang of guilt
Which conscience brings,
Escapes the piranha
And wasp that stings.
Lies low in the heart,
With the darker things.
Then rises on
A Judas with wings.
Brings you face to face
With the King of Kings.

A Closer Look

You face another mountain
Here before your eyes—
But with the great and mighty Spirit,
You'll take it by surprise.
The last one took its toll—
But now your faith is doubled.
The Lord has been so faithful—
Don't ever let your heart be troubled.

The Lord is on His way.
You're going to see a better day.
No matter what the world may say,
I know you're going to see a better day.
For the Lord your God will prepare a way.

Take a look in Jesus' eyes,
See the plans He has for you.
The evil one will disguise
The blessings in store for you.

Take a look at the mountain.
At first glance there seems no way.
It's so dark and so uncertain.
Jesus will light the way.

One Day, I'll Pray

The house is quiet and lonely,
My mind is lost, in a TV show.
I can hear Jesus beckoning,
But I just can't find the strength or will.
As I watch my favorite episode,
I can feel my heart slowly losing ground.
I can still hear Him calling me,
He won't give up, and I won't give in.

One day, I'll pray.
One day, I'll be okay.
One day, I'll get down on my knees.
One day, I'll pray.
One day, but not today.
I just can't find the time today.

At The Altar

At the altar I find peace
That passes all understanding.
I find Jesus and His cleansing blood
That sets me free.

My problems seem so small.
His love for me is so great.
My sins are forgiven
By His omnipresent grace.

At the Altar, my purpose is clear.
No fear or doubt can conquer me there.
His reassuring hand in mine
Gives me strength to take the call.

I know I can't go wrong
When He's right there by my side.
I kneel in effort
To emaciate my pride.

I know what I find at the altar
I can take home with me.
I don't ever have to be alone.
I can take Jesus wherever I go.

Chapter Four

DEATH

Rogna

As I drive this road, my heart is heavy.
I'm sad you are gone, though now you are free.
These visions I saw and allied to thee:

Nineteen vultures on a skeleton tree—
Nineteen against one—you fought gracefully.
Countless sunflowers line two-eighty-three—
One for each smile you create, cannily.
Five turns of the wheel in this old Chevy—
One for each year you instructed me.
One rising red sun—chasing me to the sea—
Someday too soon it will catch even me.

We gather in joy remembering you,
We gather in tears sorely missing you.
Your family is so very proud of you.
Your mother, a gem, we hold tenderly.
Your father, a novel, we read proudly.
Your daughter will uphold your legacy.
Your grandchildren honor your memory.
In Heaven, David, now comforts you.
Your casket I bear with humility.

Sadness

Sadness crept
Into my day,
Like long
White cirrus,
Thickening,
Gray.

The Day Bill Teegins Died

The Day Bill Teegins died,
An airplane fell quite furious
From a sky still mystified—
O State forlorn—delirious.

A fiery crash near Denver,
With nine dear friends beside—
A sporting nation cried.

Just hours before the crash,
His play-by-play voice singing—
Even as defeat was stinging.

Time stopped in Oklahoma
'til all who knew them cried—
Gates of heaven open wide.

Dust And Ashes

Thoughts of ending return to me,
Thoughts all they are, until you believe.
Knowing the road ahead lies rough.
Wondering if I'll be man enough.

Like a grasshopper on a hook in a creek.
The fish looms large, its situation bleak.
The fisherman tugs, makes the grasshopper kick.
The fish takes notice as the seconds tick.

A voice in the wind drifts to his ear,
"Supper is ready, my darling dear."
The fisherman reels, the fish swims by.
The grasshopper is left on the hook to die.

Life seems so cruel, but seldom it is.
After all, we were not, but dust and ashes.
Every experience, be it wonderful or sad,
Is a miracle of life, just waiting to be had.

Gods And Generals

I watched a little girl
Struggle to comprehend
The concept of civil war
While watching the movie
Gods And Generals.
Stonewall Jackson's ghost
Peered over our shoulders,
Still proclaiming that that
Term belonged to the line,
Not to him. The little girl
Ran off down the hallway
And turned the light on
In the back bedroom.
Her ghost was a gentle one—
Still searching for her father.

Is Death So Sweet

Is death so sweet
It cannot wait
The natural course
Of love and hate?

Is life not worth
The pain you share
With loved ones dear?
You know they care.

Please wait a while,
Let fires retreat.
Let pain dissolve,
Let love secrete.

Peace In Loss

I loathe the moth that hovers near,
Its life when lost, is my peace gained.
When one moth dies, three more appear,
My peace now lost, though just attained—
The dead moth though, its peace remained.

The blue light glows so temptingly
To those who wish to irritate.
While I compose this symphony,
The foolish fly towards ill fate—
My heart found peace through bitter hate.

Life burdens on, loved ones depart—
They're led on t'wards that glowing light.
They find the peace that's in their heart,
While we stay here to mourn and fight—
To make our way through earthly blight.

Dead Time

Part One

My brother had just passed away
The afternoon before. He was sixteen.
I lay on the floor in his bedroom,
Crying, inconsolable. I was ten.
I could hear Floyd Cramer's
Last Date playing on the eight track.
I drifted into nightmares,
Halfway listening to the mourners
That had gathered bringing
Food and well meaning prayers.
I dreamed that someone
Was pinching my arm.
I woke up alarmed, no one was there.
My arm hurt where I had
Dreamed it had been pinched.
I started crying again.
I think my brother was just saying goodbye.
Melba saw me crying, came in the room
and hugged me—she sat a while with me,
Told me everything would be okay,
That God had a special plan for me.

Dead Time

Part Two

I had just laid my head down,
Sleeping on the living room floor
Of my friend's trailer house—
Wendell and I were going hiking the next morning.
He was already asleep in the bedroom
On the other side of the kitchen.
I heard footsteps slowly creeping
Across the kitchen floor, stop,
Then creep back across the kitchen
To the bedroom where he was sleeping.
I thought I had awakened him when I came in,
And that he had come into the kitchen
To make sure it was me.
In a couple of minutes, I heard more footsteps,
This time it was Wendell,
He asked me if I had looked
Into his bedroom a minute ago—
Of course I had not. Chills ran through my body.
I had awakened something else—
The strange, curious spirit
Of the trailer house
Was checking in on us both.

Casualties Of Impatience

Edward Ray Huling, November 16, 1963-September 13, 1980.

Casualties of impatience, unanswerable equations.
Complexities intricately woven in simplicity.
Eternal consequences, asphalt and barbed wire fences.
Dreams lost in the fabric of congealed senses.

He was just sixteen. Eddie was tall and lean.
He was driving Joe's old tractor to the south pasture.
An oilfield truck in a rush to deliver—
Crashed into Eddie with a chilling shiver.
The tractor flipped over on top of our brother.
No time to think, no time to see mother.
In the red dirt and sandburs, he thought out his last words.
The smell of diesel and asphalt impaired his senses.
His last sight was filled with barbed wire fences—
With no one there who cared, just an oilfield driver impaired.
All the dreams he had of being a forest ranger—
All the people in town with no idea of the danger—
The billion what ifs that were lost in the sea—
Nothing could stop the obtuse catastrophe.

He was a casualty of impatience, an unanswerable equation.
A complexity, intricately woven in simplicity.

Stained Glass Heart

Fragile, my soul is—
Weakened by the winter freeze,
Waiting for summer.

Through this stained glass heart,
Summer's long rays emanate—
Warming winter's snow.

Edwards Brothers,Inc!
Thorofare, NJ 08086
04 January, 2011
BA2011004